What the Romans Did for the World

Alison Hawes

Crabtree Publishing Company
www.crabtreebooks.com

Author: Alison Hawes
Editor: Crystal Sikkens
Project coordinator: Kathy Middleton
Production coordinator: Ken Wright
Prepress technician: Margaret Amy Salter
Series consultant: Gill Matthews

Picture credits:
Alamy: Don Tonge 17b
Bridgeman Art Library: Museo e Gallerie Nazionali di Capodimonte, Naples, Italy, Lauros/Giraudon 6
Dreamstime: Rafael Laguillo 4, Kati Neudert 14b
Shutterstock: (Cover) Malibu Books, Elena Elisseeva, Kate Linesz, Jasenka Luksa; Chad Bontrager 15b, Joseph Calev 16-17, Franck Camhi 21, Jacek Chabraszewski 9b, Stephen Coburn 12, Anna Dzondzua 10, Elena Elisseeva 14-15, Helen & Vlad Filatov 11t, Liv Friis-Larsen 9tcl, Laurence Gough 18, George Green 13, Margo Harrison 9tl, Tomo Jesenicnik 9tr, Verity Johnson 8, Anne Kitzman 19, Jasenka Luksa 20, Zaichenko Olga 11bl, PhotoCreate 7, Tatiana Popova 16bl, Rainbow 5, Jack Scrivener 11bc, Radovan Spurny 9tcr, Margaret M Stewart 11br, Ultimathule 16br

Library and Archives Canada Cataloguing in Publication

Hawes, Alison, 1952-
    What the Romans did for the world / Alison Hawes.

(Crabtree connections)
Includes index.
ISBN 978-0-7787-9943-6 (bound).--ISBN 978-0-7787-9965-8 (pbk.)

    1. Civilization--Roman influences--Juvenile literature. 2. Rome --Civilization--Juvenile literature. 3. Rome--History--Juvenile literature. I. Title. II. Series: Crabtree connections

DG77.H39 2010   j937   C2010-901510-X

Library of Congress Cataloging-in-Publication Data

Hawes, Alison, 1952-
    What the Romans did for the world / Alison Hawes.
        p. cm. -- (Crabtree connections)
    Includes index.
    ISBN 978-0-7787-9943-6 (reinforced lib. bdg. : alk. paper)
    -- ISBN 978-0-7787-9965-8 (pbk. : alk. paper)
    1. Rome--Civilization--Influence--Juvenile literature. 2. Civilization--Roman influences--Juvenile literature. 3. Rome--History--Juvenile literature. I. Title. II. Series.

DG77.H354 2010
937--dc22
                                                    2010008054

Crabtree Publishing Company

www.crabtreebooks.com   1-800-387-7650

Printed in the U.S.A./062010/WO20100815

Published in Canada
Crabtree Publishing
616 Welland Ave.
St. Catharines, Ontario
L2M 5V6

Published in the United States
Crabtree Publishing
PMB 59051
350 Fifth Avenue, 59th Floor
New York, New York 10118

Contents

The Romans and Celts

The Romans came from Rome in Italy. They had a big, strong army that **conquered** a lot of countries, including Britain. The changes the Romans brought to Britain spread throughout the world.

Roman invasion

About 2,000 years ago, the Romans conquered England, Wales, and parts of Scotland. People called the Celts lived in Britain when the Romans **invaded**. The Romans **ruled** the Celts for 400 years.

The Roman Empire was ruled by an emperor. This is a statue of Emperor Nero.

The Romans and the Celts were very different people. They:

- [ ] wore different clothes
- [ ] spoke different languages
- [ ] ate different foods
- [ ] lived in different kinds of houses
- [ ] had different ideas about how to live

When the Romans came, they brought their different ways with them.

The Celts lived in simple, wooden houses like this one. Roman houses were larger and made of stone or brick.

Language

The Romans did not speak the same language as the Celts. The Romans spoke a language called Latin. When the Romans conquered Britain, some Celts also learned how to speak Latin.

A Roman girl learns to read and write

Latin today

Today, many languages in the world use words that come from Latin. Many children also have Latin names. ....

DO YOU HAVE A LATIN NAME?
Amanda Dominic Mica
Anthony Stacy

Teaching the Celts

Before the Romans came, the Celts did not read or write. The Romans taught rich and important Celts to read and write in Latin.

A B C D E F G H I

Ɐ ꓭ Ɔ D Ǝ ꓞ Ø Z H Ɵ

Our alphabet (top) is similar to the Roman alphabet (bottom).

The word "library" comes from the Latin word *liber*, which means "book."

Food

The Celts were farmers. They raised animals for food, leather, and wool. They grew food such as beans, peas, and wheat. They cooked food on a fire on the floor of their house.

Roman diet

The Romans ate different food from the Celts. The Romans brought these new foods to Britain.

Roman plates and spoons

The Romans did not eat with knives and forks. They used a spoon and their fingers.

Apples

Cherries

Chicken

Pears

Takeout meal

Some Romans bought hot food from shops and street **vendors**. This was a new idea to the Celts. Today, we buy takeout food just like the Romans did.

Many Romans ate burgers just like we do today.

Make a Roman burger

1. Mix 1 pound (0.45 kg) of ground beef with pine nuts, salt, and 1 tbsp (15 ml) of beef stock.

2. Mold into four round, flat patties and fry until cooked.

9

Roads

When the Romans came to Britain, the soldiers built 10,000 miles (16,000 km) of roads. They wanted straight roads so the army could travel quickly from place to place.

Most Roman roads were very straight.

Built to last

Roman roads were well made. They lasted for hundreds of years. Many modern roads in Britain are built on top of old Roman roads.

ROMAN ROAD NAMES

The word in Latin for "road" is via. Sometimes a main road was named after the emperor. Some common road names were Via Claudia and Via Traina.

Modern roads are smooth. Romans had a bumpy ride on their stone and log roads!

DID YOU KNOW?

Roman carts had to drive on the left-hand side of the road. British people still drive on the left-hand side of the road.

Trade roads

Good roads made it easier for the Celts to travel and **trade** with the Romans.

The Celts sold many things to the Romans.

Wheat

Hunting dogs

Silver

Towns

The Celts lived on farms and in villages before the Romans invaded. The Romans were used to living in towns with markets and stores. They built many new towns in Britain.

The same layout

Most Roman towns were built using the same plan. A big square, called a **forum**, was built in the middle of the town. Walls were built around the town.

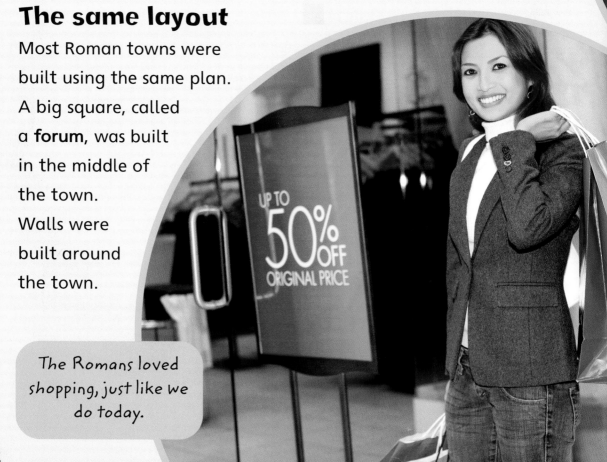

The Romans loved shopping, just like we do today.

A town below!

Many British towns are built on top of towns that were first built by the Romans.

The British city of York was built by the Romans.

LONDINIUM

The Latin name for the city of London was Londinium. It was an important trading center for the Romans.

In Britain, the names of many Roman towns end in "chester," "cester," or "caster." These endings come from the Latin word *castra* meaning "camp."

Baths

The Romans liked to keep clean. They built public baths in many towns. This was a new idea.

Transporting water

The Romans made sure every town had clean, fresh water. They dug wells and built **aqueducts** to bring water from the hills to the towns.

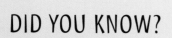

Aqueducts were made of stone.

The British city of Bath is named for the baths the Romans built there.

Keeping clean

The Romans did not have soap. Instead, they put oil on their skin. A **slave** took the oil and the dirt off with a scraper.

ROMAN BATHS HAD MANY ROOMS:

- Some were very hot
- Some were very cold
- Some were just warm

Toilets

The Romans built public toilets in Britain. This was a new idea. Rich Romans also built toilets in their own homes.

No privacy!

Roman toilets were not private. There were no doors to close. People sat next to each other and could talk to their friends if they wanted!

DID YOU KNOW?

The Romans did not use toilet paper. Instead they used a sponge on a stick.

These holes cut into stone were Roman public toilets. Sixteen people could use them at the same time!

Clean toilets

Some Roman toilets had water running underneath them to keep them clean. Sewer pipes took the dirty water away.

Some Roman toilets were free, but some were not. Public toilets in North America are free, but Europe still has some pay toilets, like the one shown here.

Homes

The Celts lived in round houses made from wood or stone. They had just one room and a **thatched** roof of straw or reeds.

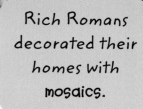

Rich Romans decorated their homes with mosaics.

Roman houses

Roman houses were different shapes. Some had many rooms. Sometimes they had more than one **story**.

Town or country?

Wealthy Romans built homes called villas in the country. Some rich Celts also built villas in the country.

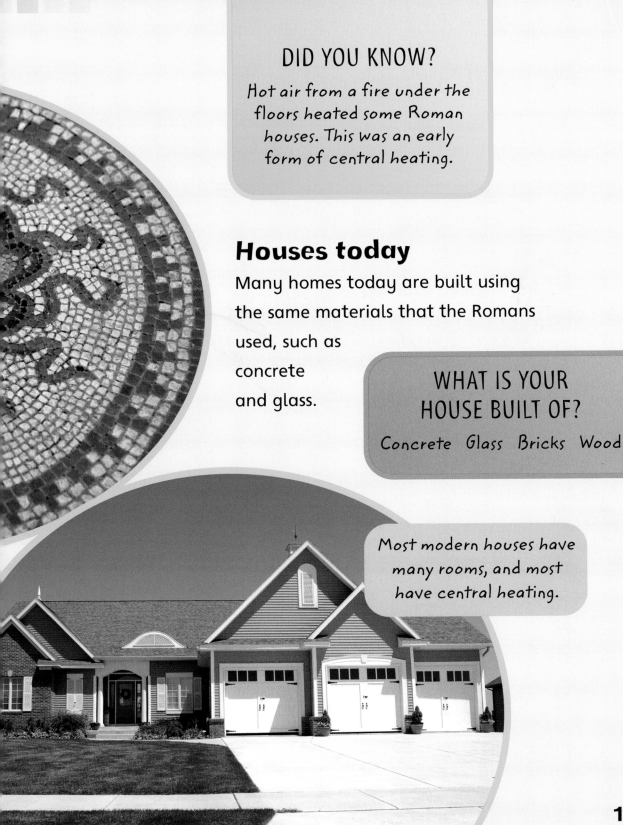

DID YOU KNOW?

Hot air from a fire under the floors heated some Roman houses. This was an early form of central heating.

Houses today

Many homes today are built using the same materials that the Romans used, such as concrete and glass.

WHAT IS YOUR HOUSE BUILT OF?

Concrete Glass Bricks Wood

Most modern houses have many rooms, and most have central heating.

Numbers

Instead of the numbers we use today, Romans used letters to write their numbers. Some numbers were very long. For example, the number 738 looked like this: DCCXXXVIII.

Letter	Number
I	1
V	5
X	10
L	50
C	100
D	500
M	1,000

In Roman numerals each letter stands for a certain number. Grouping letters together creates different numbers.

Many clocks and watches people use today have Roman numerals.

Counting people

The Romans counted the number of people who lived in the empire. They called this a **census**. In the United States and Canada, there is a census every ten years.

Roman calendar

The Romans also gave us our calendar. Like the Romans, we have seven days in a week, 365 days in a year, and 366 days in a **leap year**.

21

Glossary

aqueduct A pipe or channel for carrying water

census A count of the number of people living in one place

conquer To overcome an enemy

forum A Roman market square with stores and public buildings

invade To attack another country with an army

leap year Every four years, a year has an extra day

mosaic A picture made from tiny pieces of glass or stone

rule To be in charge of

slave A person forced to work for little or no pay

story A level of a building that is above its ground floor

thatched Straw or grass woven to make a roof

trade To buy and sell goods

vendor Someone who sells goods

Further Information

Web sites

Learn about some of the greatest achievements of the ancient Romans at:
www.roman-empire.net/children/achieve.html

Find out about the Roman invasion of Britain and how people traveled at the Web site of the British Broadcasting Corporation (BBC):
www.bbc.co.uk/schools/romans/invasion/
www.bbc.co.uk/schools/primaryhistory/romans/roads_and_places/

Discover how the Romans first conquered and then shaped the history of the people of Britain at:
www.resourcesforhistory.com

Books

The Romans in Britain (Tracking Down) by Moira Butterfield. Franklin Watts (2010)

Romans (Ancients in Their Own Words) by Michael Kerrigan. Benchmark Books (2010)

Romans: Dress, Eat, Write and Play just like the Romans (Hands-On History) by Fiona Macdonald. Crabtree Publishing Company (2008)

Life of the Ancient Celts (Peoples of the Ancient World) by Hazel Richardson. Crabtree Publishing Company (2005)

Life in Ancient Rome (Peoples of the Ancient World) by Shilpa Mehta-Jones. Crabtree Publishing Company (2005)

Index